TABLE OF CONTENTS

Acknowledgments

In the vast landscape of life, where challenges and opportunities intertwine, the pursuit of success becomes a dynamic journey—an intricate dance of strategy, resilience, and self-discovery. "Strategic

Ascendance: Crafting Your Path to Success" by Paulo Gonçalves invites you to embark on this transformative expedition, where the art of influence and the mastery of strategic thinking converge.

In a world teeming with possibilities, the need for a roadmap to success has never been more pronounced. This book emerges as your compass, guiding you through the complexities of modern existence and revealing the timeless principles that shape the ascendance of those who dare to dream big.

As you delve into these pages, you'll find more than just a compilation of strategies; you'll discover a philosophy—an empowering perspective that transcends the conventional boundaries of achievement. The journey to success, after all, is not a linear path but a tapestry woven with threads of innovation, adaptability, and perseverance.

"Strategic Ascendance" distills the essence of strategic thinking, providing insights that transcend industries, professions, and personal aspirations. It is a playbook for those who aspire not just to succeed, but to ascend strategically—to carve their niche in a world that demands ingenuity and foresight.

The principles outlined within these chapters are not mandates but invitations—to explore, to question, and to adapt. In the pursuit of your aspirations, may you find inspiration within these words, and may they serve as a catalyst for your unique journey toward strategic ascendance.

Here's to crafting your path to success—a journey that goes beyond the ordinary and ushers you into the realm of strategic mastery.

Best wishes on your ascent,

Paulo Gonçalves Author, "Strategic Ascendance: Crafting Your Path to Success"

Chapter 1: Foundations of Strategic Thinking

Section 1: Understanding Strategic Mindsets

In the dynamic tapestry of success, the cornerstone is laid by strategic thinking—a mindset that transcends the ordinary and charts a course for ascendancy. This section delves into the essence of strategic mindsets, unraveling the intricacies that distinguish strategic thinkers in the pursuit of greatness.

1.1 The Evolution of Strategy

As we embark on this exploration, it is imperative to trace the lineage of strategic thought. From the battlefield maneuvers of ancient generals to the boardrooms of contemporary visionaries, the evolution of strategy reveals timeless principles that resonate across diverse landscapes. By understanding the historical context of strategic thinking, we uncover the strategic DNA that has withstood the test of time.

1.2 Cultivating a Strategic Mindset

The heart of strategic thinking lies in the cultivation of a mindset attuned to the nuances of complexity and opportunity. Strategic thinkers possess a unique blend of traits that enable them to navigate ambiguity with finesse. Foresight, adaptability, and a keen understanding of the interconnectedness of variables are the building blocks of this mindset. Through practical insights and illustrative examples, we explore how these attributes can be nurtured and honed, becoming second nature to those seeking strategic ascendance.

Subsection 1.2.1: Foresight as the North Star

At the core of a strategic mindset is the ability to peer into the future with clarity. Foresight is not merely a skill; it is the North Star that guides strategic thinkers through uncertainty. This subsection dissects the components of foresight, examining how it empowers individuals to anticipate trends, identify potential obstacles, and position themselves advantageously in the unfolding narrative of their journey.

Subsection 1.2.2: Adaptability as a Strategic Imperative

Strategic thinkers embrace change as a constant companion on their journey. Adaptability is not just a response to unforeseen challenges but a proactive approach to harnessing change for strategic advantage. We delve into the art of adaptability, exploring case studies and strategies that showcase how successful individuals and organizations pivot and thrive amidst evolving circumstances.

Subsection 1.2.3: Interconnected Thinking

The strategic mindset perceives the world as an interconnected web of variables. In this subsection, we unravel the concept of interconnected thinking, emphasizing how strategic thinkers discern patterns, anticipate ripple effects, and make decisions that consider the broader landscape. Through anecdotes and analyses, we illustrate how interconnected thinking transforms challenges into opportunities for those navigating the complex terrain of success.

Understanding strategic mindsets is the first step towards unlocking the full potential of strategic thinking. As we navigate this exploration, we invite you to reflect on how these principles can illuminate your path to strategic ascendance.

Section 2: Navigating Complexity with Foresight

In the tapestry of success, woven with the threads of uncertainty and opportunity, foresight emerges as the guiding beacon for those traversing the complex landscape. This section illuminates the pivotal role of foresight in strategic thinking, unraveling the layers of anticipation, pattern recognition, and clear vision that empower individuals to navigate complexity with purpose.

1.3 The Role of Foresight in Strategic Planning

As we embark on this exploration, it becomes evident that strategic thinking is, at its core, an exercise in foresight. The ability to peer into the future, discern emerging trends, and envision potential scenarios forms the bedrock of strategic planning. In this section, we dissect the indispensable role of foresight in crafting strategic plans that stand resilient in the face of uncertainty.

Subsection 1.3.1: Anticipating Trends and Patterns

Foresight transcends mere prediction; it is an art of anticipation. By analyzing historical precedents and understanding the dynamics of change, strategic thinkers develop a keen ability to anticipate trends and recognize emerging patterns. This subsection delves into the methodologies employed by those with strategic foresight, offering insights into how one can cultivate the acumen to navigate the evolving landscape.

Subsection 1.3.2: Scenario Planning for Uncertainty

In a world characterized by volatility, uncertainty, complexity, and ambiguity (VUCA), scenario planning becomes an invaluable tool for strategic thinkers. Here, we explore the practice of envisioning multiple plausible futures, allowing individuals to prepare for a spectrum of possibilities. Through real-world examples, we illustrate how scenario planning enhances adaptability and resilience in the face of dynamic challenges.

Subsection 1.3.3: Envisioning Your Future

Foresight extends beyond a global perspective; it encompasses the personal realm. Strategic thinkers visualize their individual futures, aligning personal goals with a broader vision. This subsection encourages readers to embark on a journey of self-discovery, providing exercises and reflections to help articulate and shape personal aspirations within the context of a strategic life plan.

As we navigate the intricacies of foresight, we invite you to embrace the power of anticipation. It is through this lens that the complexity of the world transforms into a canvas of possibilities waiting to be painted by the strategic mind.

Chapter 2: The Art of Influence

Section 1: Mastering the Dynamics of Persuasion

In the intricate dance of strategic ascendance, the art of influence emerges as a formidable tool. This section delves into the nuances of persuasion, unraveling the psychology, tactics, and ethical considerations that define the strategic influencer.

2.1 The Psychology of Persuasion

At the heart of mastering persuasion lies an understanding of human psychology. In this section, we explore the cognitive and emotional factors that shape decision-making. By delving into principles such as social proof, reciprocity, and scarcity, strategic thinkers gain insights into the intricacies of the human mind, allowing them to navigate the terrain of influence with finesse.

Subsection 2.1.1: Building Credibility and Trust

Credibility is the currency of influence. Strategic influencers cultivate trust by establishing authenticity, competence, and reliability. This subsection provides a roadmap for building and maintaining credibility, exploring case studies that highlight the transformative power of trust in the realm of strategic relationships.

Subsection 2.1.2: Emotional Intelligence in Persuasion

Emotional intelligence becomes a strategic asset in the pursuit of influence. This subsection explores how an acute awareness of one's emotions and the emotions of others enhances persuasive capabilities. From empathetic communication to conflict resolution, emotional intelligence serves as the linchpin of successful persuasion.

2.2 Tactical Approaches to Influence

Persuasion is an art that demands a strategic repertoire of tactics. In this section, we delve into the tactical approaches employed by master influencers. From the subtle art of framing messages to the power of storytelling, readers are equipped with a toolkit that transcends manipulation and embraces ethical influence.

Subsection 2.2.1: The Power of Storytelling

Narrative transcends facts; it captures hearts and minds. This subsection explores how storytelling, when wielded strategically, becomes a potent tool for influence. Through analysis of impactful narratives and practical exercises, readers learn to craft compelling stories that resonate with their audience, fostering connection and persuasion.

Subsection 2.2.2: Framing and Reframing Strategies

The way information is presented shapes perception. Strategic influencers master the art of framing and reframing, skillfully positioning ideas to garner support and reshape perspectives. This subsection unveils the principles behind effective framing, offering readers insights into how to frame messages strategically for maximum impact.

In mastering the dynamics of persuasion, strategic thinkers elevate their ability to shape outcomes, build alliances, and inspire action. As we navigate this exploration, we invite you to embrace the art of influence with a conscious commitment to ethical and impactful persuasion.

Section 2: Building Lasting Connections

In the tapestry of strategic ascendance, the ability to forge lasting connections emerges as a cornerstone of influence. This section delves into the art of building meaningful relationships, exploring the dynamics, principles, and strategies that transform fleeting interactions into enduring connections.

2.3 The Dynamics of Relationship Building

Building lasting connections extends beyond transactional exchanges; it embodies the creation of mutually beneficial alliances. In this section, we dissect the dynamics of relationship building, emphasizing the principles that underpin authentic connections and sustain them over time.

Subsection 2.3.1: Authenticity and Genuine Engagement

Authenticity is the foundation upon which enduring connections are built. This subsection explores the role of authenticity in forging meaningful relationships, encouraging readers to engage genuinely with others. Through anecdotes and reflections, we illustrate how authenticity fosters trust, a bedrock of lasting connections.

Subsection 2.3.2: The Power of Empathy in Connection

Empathy is the bridge that connects individuals on a deeper level. Strategic influencers master the art of empathetic connection, understanding the perspectives and emotions of others. This subsection provides practical strategies for cultivating empathy, transforming interactions from transactional to transformative.

2.4 Strategies for Sustaining Connections

In the dynamic tapestry of life, sustaining connections requires intentionality and strategic nurturing. This section unveils strategies for ensuring the longevity of relationships, from professional networks to personal bonds.

Consistent communication is the lifeblood of lasting connections. This subsection explores the art of maintaining regular contact and strategic follow-up, ensuring that relationships remain vibrant and meaningful over time. Through actionable tips, readers gain insights into fostering connections that withstand the test of time.

Subsection 2.4.2: Reciprocity and Mutual Benefit

Reciprocity forms the heartbeat of enduring connections. This subsection delves into the principle of mutual benefit, encouraging readers to seek opportunities for collaboration and shared success. By understanding the symbiotic nature of relationships, strategic thinkers amplify the impact of their connections.

2.5 Navigating Challenges in Relationship Building

No journey of connection is without challenges. In this section, we explore common obstacles in relationship building and provide strategies for overcoming them. From navigating conflicts to managing expectations, readers gain insights into preserving and strengthening connections in the face of adversity.

As we navigate the intricacies of building lasting connections, we invite you to embark on a journey of meaningful engagement. In the realm of strategic influence, the ability to cultivate enduring connections is a powerful catalyst for personal and professional ascendance.

Chapter 3: Innovation and Adaptability

Section 1: Cultivating a Culture of Innovation

In the ever-evolving landscape of success, the ability to cultivate a culture of innovation stands as a transformative force. This section explores the principles, strategies, and mindset shifts required to foster an environment where creativity thrives, and innovation becomes a driving force for strategic ascendance.

3.1 The Essence of Innovation

At its core, innovation is more than a buzzword; it is a mindset that permeates every aspect of an organization or individual. In this section, we delve into the essence of innovation, dissecting the principles that distinguish innovative thinkers and organizations from the status quo.

Subsection 3.1.1: Embracing a Growth Mindset

A growth mindset forms the bedrock of innovation. This subsection explores how the belief in continuous learning and improvement propels individuals and organizations toward new possibilities. By cultivating a growth mindset, strategic thinkers open the door to a culture where challenges are viewed as opportunities, and failure is seen as a stepping stone to success.

Subsection 3.1.2: Creativity as a Strategic Asset

Creativity is the lifeblood of innovation. Here, we unravel the components of a creative mindset and provide practical strategies for unlocking and nurturing creativity. Through exercises and insights, readers gain tools to infuse their personal and professional endeavors with the spark of inventive thinking.

3.2 Strategies for Fostering Innovation

Cultivating a culture of innovation requires intentional strategies that go beyond encouraging creativity. This section outlines actionable approaches for fostering an environment where innovation flourishes.

Subsection 3.2.1: Encouraging Diverse Perspectives

Innovation thrives in diversity. This subsection explores the power of diverse perspectives, emphasizing the role of inclusivity in sparking innovative ideas. Through case studies and practical advice, readers gain insights into how fostering a culture of diversity contributes to a rich tapestry of ideas.

Subsection 3.2.2: Establishing a Safe Space for Experimentation

Innovation requires a degree of risk-taking and experimentation. This subsection delves into the importance of creating a safe space where individuals feel empowered to test new ideas without fear of failure. By embracing a culture that values experimentation, strategic thinkers unleash the full potential of their innovative capacity.

3.3 Integrating Innovation into Strategic Planning

Innovation is not a standalone concept but an integral component of strategic planning. This section explores how to seamlessly integrate innovation into the strategic fabric of organizations and personal pursuits.

Subsection 3.3.1: Aligning Innovation with Strategic Goals

Innovative endeavors must align with overarching strategic goals. This subsection provides insights into how strategic thinkers can ensure that innovative initiatives contribute directly to the realization of larger objectives. By intertwining innovation with strategy, individuals and organizations cultivate a dynamic and purposeful approach to success.

Subsection 3.3.2: Agile Strategies for Rapid Adaptation

In a fast-paced world, adaptability is the key to sustainable innovation. This subsection explores the principles of agile strategies, showcasing how individuals and organizations can pivot swiftly in response to changing circumstances. By integrating agility into strategic planning, strategic thinkers ensure that innovation remains a dynamic force rather than a static concept.

As we navigate the landscape of cultivating a culture of innovation, we invite you to embrace the transformative power of creative thinking. In the realm of strategic ascendance, innovation is not merely a concept; it is the engine that propels individuals and organizations toward new horizons.

Section 2: Embracing Change and Adapting Strategically

In the dynamic symphony of success, the ability to embrace change and adapt strategically emerges as a defining trait of those on the path to strategic ascendance. This section explores the principles, mindset shifts, and actionable strategies required to not only weather the winds of change but to harness them as propellors of growth and innovation.

3.4 The Nature of Change

Change is an inevitable force that shapes the trajectory of individuals and organizations. In this section, we delve into the nature of change, unraveling its intricacies and providing insights into why a proactive embrace of change is fundamental for those seeking strategic ascendance.

Subsection 3.4.1: Understanding the Dynamics of Change

Change is not a singular event but a constant force in the tapestry of life. This subsection explores the dynamics of change, from gradual shifts to disruptive transformations. By understanding the various facets of change, strategic thinkers gain the foresight to anticipate, navigate, and leverage these shifts strategically.

Subsection 3.4.2: Overcoming Resistance to Change

Resistance often accompanies change, and overcoming it is integral to adapting strategically. This subsection explores the psychological and organizational factors that contribute to resistance and provides practical strategies for fostering a mindset that embraces change as an opportunity rather than a threat.

3.5 Strategies for Strategic Adaptation

Adaptability is not merely about reacting to change but strategically navigating it to one's advantage. This section outlines actionable strategies for cultivating a mindset of strategic adaptation, ensuring that change becomes a catalyst for growth rather than a hindrance.

Subsection 3.5.1: Building a Flexible Mindset

A flexible mindset forms the cornerstone of strategic adaptation. This subsection explores the components of flexibility, from a willingness to learn to the ability to pivot when necessary. Through case studies and practical exercises, readers gain tools to cultivate a mindset that thrives in the face of uncertainty.

Subsection 3.5.2: Proactive Change Management

Strategic thinkers do not merely react to change; they manage it proactively. This subsection provides insights into proactive change management strategies, emphasizing the importance of scenario planning, continuous learning, and staying ahead of the curve. By adopting proactive change management, individuals and organizations position themselves as architects of their destiny rather than passive recipients of change.

3.6 Integrating Adaptability into Decision-Making

Adaptability extends beyond a mindset; it is a guiding principle in decision-making. This section explores how strategic thinkers can integrate adaptability into their decision-making processes, ensuring that choices align with the evolving landscape and contribute to long-term success.

Subsection 3.6.1: Adaptive Decision-Making Frameworks

Decision-making frameworks that embrace adaptability empower strategic thinkers to make informed choices in dynamic environments. This subsection introduces adaptive decision-making frameworks, providing readers with tools to assess risks, anticipate outcomes, and make decisions that align with the principles of strategic adaptation.

Subsection 3.6.2: Learning from Failure and Iterating Strategically

Failure is not a roadblock but a stepping stone on the path to success. This subsection explores the art of learning from failure, iterating strategies based on feedback, and incorporating lessons into the decision-making process. By embracing failure as a natural part of the journey, strategic thinkers ensure that setbacks become springboards for future achievements.

As we navigate the realm of embracing change and adapting strategically, we invite you to view change not as a challenge to be endured, but as a dynamic force to be harnessed for strategic ascendance. In a world of constant evolution, adaptability is not just a skill; it is the compass that guides strategic thinkers toward new horizons.

Chapter 4: Resilience in the Face of Challenges

Section 1: Overcoming Adversity with Strategic Resilience

In the tapestry of strategic ascendance, resilience stands as a formidable ally, empowering individuals to navigate challenges and emerge stronger on the other side. This section delves into the principles, mindset shifts, and strategic approaches that define resilience, showcasing how adversity can be not just endured but strategically overcome.

4.1 The Nature of Adversity

Adversity is an inevitable companion on the journey to success. In this section, we explore the nature of adversity, dissecting its various forms and recognizing it not as an obstacle to be avoided, but as a transformative force that can shape character and fuel strategic ascendance.

Subsection 4.1.1: Recognizing and Understanding Adversity

Adversity wears many faces, from unexpected setbacks to formidable challenges. This subsection encourages readers to recognize and understand the nature of adversity in their personal and professional lives. By embracing adversity as a natural part of the journey, strategic thinkers can shift their perspective and approach challenges with a strategic mindset.

Subsection 4.1.2: The Resilience Mindset

Resilience is not merely a reaction to adversity; it is a mindset that shapes responses and actions. This subsection explores the components of the resilience mindset, from optimism and adaptability to a belief in one's capacity to overcome challenges. By cultivating a resilience mindset, individuals can proactively approach adversity with a strategic orientation.

4.2 Strategies for Strategic Resilience

Strategic resilience goes beyond bouncing back from setbacks; it involves a deliberate and strategic approach to overcoming adversity. This section outlines actionable strategies for cultivating and leveraging resilience in the face of challenges.

Subsection 4.2.1: Building a Resilient Support Network

Resilience is often fortified by a strong support network. This subsection explores the importance of building resilient connections with mentors, colleagues, and friends. Through case studies and practical advice, readers gain insights into how a robust support network can serve as a strategic resource during challenging times.

Subsection 4.2.2: Learning and Growth through Adversity

Adversity is a crucible that forges learning and growth. This subsection encourages individuals to view adversity not just as a hurdle to overcome but as an opportunity for development. By extracting lessons from challenging experiences, strategic thinkers position themselves to grow strategically and apply newfound insights to future endeavors.

4.3 Navigating Crisis with Strategic Resilience

Crisis moments test the mettle of strategic thinkers. This section explores how strategic resilience can be a guiding force in navigating crises, providing a roadmap for turning challenges into strategic opportunities.

Subsection 4.3.1: Crisis Management Strategies

Crisis management requires a blend of strategic thinking and resilience. This subsection introduces crisis management strategies that empower individuals to respond strategically to unforeseen challenges. From effective communication to resource allocation, strategic resilience becomes a compass in navigating the storm of crises.

Subsection 4.3.2: Turning Setbacks into Strategic Pivots

Setbacks need not be roadblocks; they can serve as strategic pivots. This subsection showcases examples of individuals and organizations that turned adversity into an opportunity for transformation. By strategically pivoting in the face of setbacks, strategic thinkers demonstrate the power of resilience in creating new paths to success.

As we explore the realm of overcoming adversity with strategic resilience, we invite you to embrace challenges not as insurmountable obstacles, but as strategic moments that can propel you toward greater heights. In the crucible of adversity, strategic resilience becomes a beacon, guiding individuals on the path to enduring success.

Section 2: Learning from Setbacks and Moving Forward

Setbacks are not the end but a strategic juncture—a point of reflection and potential growth. This section explores the transformative power of setbacks, showcasing how strategic thinkers can navigate these moments, extract valuable lessons, and propel themselves forward on the journey to strategic ascendance.

4.4 The Strategic Value of Setbacks

Setbacks are not failures; they are opportunities for strategic recalibration. In this section, we delve into the strategic value of setbacks, illuminating how these moments can serve as catalysts for learning, growth, and a renewed sense of purpose.

Subsection 4.4.1: Reframing Setbacks as Learning Opportunities

The way setbacks are framed shapes their impact on the journey. This subsection explores the art of reframing setbacks as valuable learning opportunities. By shifting the perspective from failure to feedback, strategic thinkers position themselves to extract insights that can inform future strategies.

Subsection 4.4.2: The Role of Reflection in Strategic Learning

Reflection is a powerful tool in the arsenal of strategic learners. This subsection emphasizes the importance of introspection and reflection following setbacks. Through guided exercises and case studies, readers are encouraged to embrace reflection as a strategic practice, extracting deeper insights from challenging experiences.

4.5 Strategies for Strategic Learning and Adaptation

Moving forward from setbacks involves intentional strategies for learning and adaptation. This section outlines actionable approaches for strategic thinkers to assimilate lessons, adjust strategies, and emerge stronger from setbacks.

Subsection 4.5.1: Developing a Continuous Learning Mindset

Continuous learning is a strategic mindset that transforms setbacks into stepping stones. This subsection explores the principles of continuous learning and provides practical strategies for cultivating a mindset that thrives on curiosity, adaptability, and a hunger for knowledge. By embracing a continuous learning mindset, strategic thinkers position themselves to navigate challenges with resilience and agility.

Subsection 4.5.2: Iterative Strategies for Ongoing Improvement

Strategic adaptation involves an iterative approach to strategy. This subsection introduces the concept of iterative strategies, emphasizing the importance of ongoing improvement. Through case studies and actionable advice, readers gain insights into how to iteratively refine their approaches based on feedback, ensuring that setbacks become pivotal moments in a journey of strategic ascendance.

4.6 Strategic Resurgence and Future Success

Setbacks need not define the future; they can serve as springboards for strategic resurgence. This section explores the concept of strategic resurgence, showcasing how individuals and organizations can emerge from setbacks with renewed vigor, clarity, and a strategic vision for the future.

Subsection 4.6.1: Realigning Goals with Strategic Vision

Strategic resurgence involves realigning goals with a strategic vision for the future. This subsection provides guidance on how to reassess and refine goals in the aftermath of setbacks, ensuring that they remain aligned with the overarching strategic vision. By integrating setbacks into the strategic narrative, individuals position themselves for future success.

Subsection 4.6.2: Leveraging Setbacks for Innovation and Creativity

Setbacks can be catalysts for innovation and creativity. This subsection explores how strategic thinkers can leverage setbacks as opportunities to innovate and create. Through case studies and practical exercises, readers gain insights into how to foster a culture where setbacks fuel creative thinking and inspire strategic solutions.

As we explore the journey of learning from setbacks and moving forward, we invite you to view setbacks not as detours but as strategic waypoints on the path to enduring success. In the realm of strategic ascendance, setbacks become the raw material for resilience, adaptation, and a future defined by strategic triumphs.

Chapter 5: Crafting Your Unique Strategy

Section 1: Defining Your Vision and Mission

At the core of strategic ascendance lies the articulation of a compelling vision and mission — the guiding stars that illuminate the path to success. This section explores the foundational elements of vision and mission, providing insights, strategies, and practical exercises for individuals and organizations seeking to carve their unique strategic identity.

5.1 The Strategic Significance of Vision and Mission

Vision and mission are not mere statements; they are the bedrock upon which strategic success is built. In this section, we delve into the strategic significance of defining a clear vision and mission, showcasing how these elements serve as the north stars that guide strategic thinkers on their journey.

Subsection 5.1.1: The Role of Vision in Strategic Direction

Vision is the panoramic view of the future that inspires and directs. This subsection explores the role of vision in providing strategic direction, emphasizing how a well-crafted vision statement becomes a rallying point for individuals and organizations. Through case studies and reflective exercises, readers gain insights into the process of crafting a vision that transcends the ordinary and ignites the flames of strategic ambition.

Subsection 5.1.2: Mission as the Strategic Blueprint

Mission is the strategic blueprint that outlines the purpose and activities of an individual or organization. This subsection delves into the components of a compelling mission statement, showcasing how it aligns with the vision to create a cohesive and impactful strategic narrative.

Through practical exercises, readers embark on the journey of crafting a mission that not only defines purpose but also informs strategic decision-making.

5.2 Crafting a Compelling Vision

Crafting a compelling vision requires a blend of inspiration and strategic foresight. This section outlines actionable strategies for individuals and organizations to articulate a vision that encapsulates their aspirations and sets the stage for strategic ascendance.

Subsection 5.2.1: Inspiring and Aspirational Language

A compelling vision is expressed through inspiring and aspirational language. This subsection explores the power of words in crafting a vision that resonates with stakeholders and instills a sense of purpose. By delving into the art of language, readers gain tools to infuse their vision statements with emotional resonance and strategic impact.

Subsection 5.2.2: Aligning Personal Values with Vision

A vision that aligns with personal values possesses an authentic and enduring quality. This subsection guides individuals through the process of aligning their personal values with their strategic vision. Through self-reflection and exercises, readers gain clarity on the values that will serve as the foundation for their strategic journey.

5.3 Articulating a Purposeful Mission

A purposeful mission is a roadmap for strategic endeavors. This section provides strategies and insights into the process of articulating a mission statement that succinctly captures the essence of an individual or organization's purpose and activities.

Subsection 5.3.1: Defining Core Competencies and Activities

A mission statement is strengthened by a clear definition of core competencies and activities. This subsection explores how individuals and organizations can identify their unique strengths and capabilities, shaping a mission that leverages these assets strategically. Through practical exercises, readers gain insights into defining the activities that will propel them toward their strategic objectives.

Subsection 5.3.2: Incorporating Adaptability into Mission Statements

In a dynamic world, adaptability is a strategic imperative. This subsection guides readers on how to incorporate adaptability into their mission statements, ensuring that the mission remains relevant and resilient in the face of changing circumstances. By embracing adaptability, individuals and organizations infuse their missions with the flexibility needed for sustained success.

As we embark on the journey of defining vision and mission, we invite you to consider these elements not as static statements but as dynamic forces that guide and evolve with the strategic narrative. In crafting your vision and mission, you set the compass for strategic ascendance, charting a course that aligns passion with purpose and ambition with strategic clarity.

Section 2: Developing a Strategic Plan for Success

A vision and mission serve as the guiding stars, but a strategic plan transforms aspirations into actionable steps toward success. This section delves into the art and science of developing a strategic plan, offering insights, methodologies, and practical frameworks for individuals and organizations committed to realizing their strategic vision.

5.4 The Blueprint of Strategic Planning

Strategic planning is the blueprint that transforms vision and mission into a roadmap for success. In this section, we explore the foundational elements of strategic planning, shedding light on the strategic thinking and decision-making processes that lay the groundwork for effective execution.

Subsection 5.4.1: Aligning Goals with Vision and Mission

Goals are the building blocks of a strategic plan, and their alignment with the vision and mission is paramount. This subsection provides strategies for aligning goals with the overarching vision and mission, ensuring a cohesive and purposeful approach to strategic planning. Through guided exercises, readers gain tools to articulate goals that harmonize with the strategic narrative.

Subsection 5.4.2: Establishing Key Performance Indicators (KPIs)

Measuring success is integral to strategic planning, and key performance indicators (KPIs) serve as the compass for progress. This subsection delves into the establishment of KPIs, guiding individuals and organizations in selecting metrics that align with strategic objectives. By understanding the strategic significance of each indicator, readers gain insights into how KPIs drive performance and inform strategic decision-making.

5.5 Crafting Strategic Initiatives and Action Plans

A strategic plan comes to life through well-defined initiatives and action plans. This section provides actionable strategies for crafting initiatives that propel individuals and organizations toward their strategic goals.

Subsection 5.5.1: Designing Strategic Initiatives for Impact

Strategic initiatives are the vehicles that drive progress. This subsection explores the principles of designing initiatives that create meaningful impact. Through case studies and practical advice, readers gain insights into how to prioritize initiatives, allocate resources strategically, and ensure alignment with overarching strategic goals.

Subsection 5.5.2: Developing Action Plans for Implementation

Action plans are the executional roadmap of a strategic plan. This subsection guides readers through the process of developing action plans that translate strategic goals into actionable steps. By incorporating timelines, responsibilities, and milestones, individuals and organizations ensure that their strategic initiatives progress with clarity and purpose.

5.6 Anticipating and Mitigating Risks

In the landscape of strategic planning, risks are inevitable. This section explores the strategic importance of anticipating and mitigating risks to ensure the resilience and success of the plan.

Subsection 5.6.1: Risk Assessment and Scenario Planning

A comprehensive risk assessment is foundational to strategic planning. This subsection introduces the concept of risk assessment and scenario planning, guiding individuals and organizations in identifying potential challenges and developing strategies for mitigating risks. By adopting a proactive stance toward risks, strategic thinkers enhance the adaptability and resilience of their plans.

Subsection 5.6.2: Contingency Planning for Strategic Resilience

Contingency planning is the strategic insurance against unexpected challenges. This subsection provides insights into developing contingency plans that empower individuals and organizations to respond swiftly and effectively to unforeseen circumstances. By embedding contingency planning into the strategic process, strategic thinkers position themselves to navigate disruptions with strategic resilience.

As we delve into the realm of developing a strategic plan for success, we invite you to view the planning process not as a rigid framework but as a dynamic and adaptive tool for realizing your vision and mission. In the tapestry of strategic ascendance, a well-crafted strategic plan becomes the compass that guides every step toward enduring success.

Chapter 6: Collaborative Advantage

Section 1: Building Strategic Alliances

In the intricate dance of strategic ascendance, the art of building strategic alliances emerges as a potent force that propels individuals and organizations toward collaborative advantage. This section explores the principles, strategies, and tactical considerations that define the art of forging alliances for sustained success.

6.1 The Strategic Imperative of Alliances

Strategic alliances are not merely partnerships; they are vehicles for mutual growth and success. In this section, we delve into the strategic imperative of building alliances, unraveling the profound impact that collaborative relationships can have on the strategic landscape.

Subsection 6.1.1: Recognizing Opportunities for Alliances

Opportunities for alliances abound in the dynamic tapestry of business and life. This subsection guides individuals and organizations in recognizing strategic opportunities for alliances, whether in the form of joint ventures, partnerships, or collaborative projects. Through practical insights, readers gain tools to identify potential allies and leverage shared interests for mutual benefit.

Subsection 6.1.2: Aligning Values and Objectives

Alignment is the heartbeat of successful alliances. This subsection explores the importance of aligning values and objectives with potential allies. By ensuring shared values and a common vision, strategic thinkers lay the foundation for alliances that are not only productive but also enduring. Through case studies and reflective exercises, readers gain insights into the nuanced art of alignment in the alliance-building process.

6.2 Strategies for Effective Alliance Building

Building effective alliances requires a strategic approach that goes beyond casual partnerships. This section outlines actionable strategies for individuals and organizations seeking to cultivate alliances that provide a competitive edge.

Subsection 6.2.1: Creating a Win-Win Framework

A win-win framework is the bedrock of successful alliances. This subsection provides insights into how individuals and organizations can create mutually beneficial arrangements that result in shared success. By adopting a collaborative mindset and designing partnerships that offer value to all parties, strategic thinkers position themselves for sustained advantage in the alliance landscape.

Subsection 6.2.2: Establishing Clear Communication Channels

Clear communication is the lifeblood of effective alliances. This subsection explores the role of transparent communication in alliance building, emphasizing the importance of establishing clear channels for dialogue, feedback, and collaboration. Through practical strategies, readers gain tools to foster open communication that strengthens the fabric of their alliances.

6.3 Navigating Challenges in Alliance Building

Alliances, while powerful, are not without challenges. This section explores common obstacles in alliance building and provides strategies for navigating them with finesse and strategic resilience.

Subsection 6.3.1: Managing Conflict and Disagreements

Conflict is inherent in any collaborative endeavor. This subsection delves into the art of managing conflict and disagreements in alliances, offering insights into conflict resolution strategies that preserve relationships and maintain the strategic integrity of the partnership. By viewing conflict as an opportunity for growth, strategic thinkers transform challenges into strategic opportunities.

Subsection 6.3.2: Adapting to Changing Dynamics

The strategic landscape is dynamic, and alliances must adapt to changing circumstances. This subsection explores how individuals and organizations can navigate shifting dynamics in alliances, emphasizing the importance of adaptability and proactive strategies for maintaining the relevance and effectiveness of collaborative partnerships.

As we explore the realm of building strategic alliances, we invite you to view alliances not as mere transactions but as dynamic relationships that, when nurtured strategically, become a source of enduring advantage. In the symphony of strategic ascendance, effective alliance building is the harmonious chord that resonates with collaborative advantage.

Section 2: Leveraging Networks for Success

In the tapestry of strategic ascendance, the ability to leverage networks emerges as a strategic superpower. This section delves into the principles, tactics, and transformative potential of strategically cultivating and leveraging networks for individual and collective success.

6.4 The Strategic Power of Networks

Networks are not just social connections; they are intricate webs of opportunity, knowledge, and support. In this section, we explore the strategic power inherent in networks, unraveling the layers of influence, collaboration, and growth that can be unlocked through intentional network building.

Subsection 6.4.1: Understanding the Dynamics of Networks

Networks are dynamic ecosystems shaped by relationships, trust, and reciprocity. This subsection provides insights into the dynamics of networks, exploring how individuals can navigate and leverage these interconnected spaces strategically. By understanding the principles of network dynamics, readers gain tools to navigate and harness the potential of diverse networks.

Subsection 6.4.2: Recognizing the Strategic Value of Relationships

Relationships are the currency of networks, and their strategic value extends beyond casual connections. This subsection delves into the strategic significance of relationships within networks, emphasizing the transformative power of genuine connections. Through practical advice and case studies, readers gain insights into recognizing and nurturing relationships that contribute to individual and collective success.

6.5 Strategies for Strategic Network Building

Strategic network building involves more than amassing contacts; it requires intentional cultivation and strategic engagement. This section outlines actionable strategies for individuals seeking to build and leverage networks for success.

Subsection 6.5.1: Identifying and Engaging with Key Influencers

In any network, key influencers play a pivotal role. This subsection explores how individuals can identify and strategically engage with key influencers within their networks. By understanding the power dynamics and leveraging relationships with influencers, strategic thinkers position themselves for enhanced visibility, opportunities, and collaborative ventures.

Subsection 6.5.2: Building a Diverse and Inclusive Network

The strength of a network lies in its diversity and inclusivity. This subsection provides insights into the strategic advantages of building a diverse network that encompasses individuals from varied backgrounds, industries, and perspectives. Through practical strategies, readers gain tools to foster inclusivity and tap into the richness of diverse networks.

6.6 Nurturing and Maintaining Strategic Relationships

Building a network is an ongoing process that requires nurturing and maintaining strategic relationships. This section explores the art of relationship management within networks, providing insights into how individuals can sustain meaningful connections that contribute to long-term success.

Subsection 6.6.1: Strategic Networking Events and Platforms

Strategic networking events and platforms serve as catalysts for relationship building. This subsection delves into the art of navigating and leveraging networking events, both physical and virtual, to maximize strategic connections. By adopting a proactive stance and utilizing the right platforms, individuals enhance their ability to connect with like-minded professionals and collaborators.

Subsection 6.6.2: Providing Value and Reciprocity

Reciprocity forms the foundation of successful network building. This subsection explores the importance of providing value within networks, whether through knowledge-sharing, introductions, or collaborative initiatives. By adopting a mindset of reciprocity, individuals cultivate relationships that are not only beneficial to them but contribute to the collective success of the network.

As we explore the realm of leveraging networks for success, we invite you to view networks not as static entities but as dynamic ecosystems teeming with potential. In the tapestry of strategic ascendance, strategic network building is the thread that weaves together opportunities, insights, and collaborative ventures, creating a fabric of success that extends beyond individual accomplishments.

Chapter 7: Leadership Alchemy

Section 1: Leadership Styles for Strategic Ascendance

In the orchestration of strategic ascendance, leadership emerges as the conductor, shaping the symphony of success. This section explores the diverse styles of leadership, offering insights, strategies, and reflections on how different leadership approaches can contribute to individual and collective strategic triumphs.

7.1 The Mosaic of Leadership Styles

Leadership is not a one-size-fits-all concept; it is a mosaic of styles, each contributing its unique brushstroke to the canvas of success. In this section, we delve into the various leadership styles that individuals can adopt and adapt on their journey to strategic ascendance.

Subsection 7.1.1: The Visionary Leader

Visionary leadership transcends the ordinary, painting a compelling picture of the future. This subsection explores the attributes of visionary leaders, individuals who inspire with a clear and captivating vision. Through case studies and practical insights, readers gain an understanding of how visionary leadership can serve as a catalyst for strategic ascendance.

Subsection 7.1.2: The Transformational Leader

Transformational leadership ignites change and growth at both individual and organizational levels. This subsection delves into the characteristics of transformational leaders, individuals who foster innovation, build strong relationships, and empower others to reach their full potential. Through reflective exercises, readers explore how to embody and apply transformational leadership principles on their strategic journey.

7.2 The Strategic Navigator

Strategic navigation requires a leader who can chart the course and navigate through complexities. This section explores the qualities and strategies of leaders who serve as strategic navigators, guiding individuals and organizations toward their goals with foresight and adaptability.

Subsection 7.2.1: The Analytical Strategist

Analytical strategists possess a keen ability to dissect complex scenarios and formulate data-driven strategies. This subsection explores how analytical leaders bring clarity to ambiguity, utilizing analytical thinking to inform strategic decision-making. Through practical frameworks and case studies, readers gain insights into how to cultivate an analytical mindset for strategic leadership.

Subsection 7.2.2: The Adaptive Decision Maker

Adaptive decision makers thrive in dynamic environments, adjusting their strategies to meet changing circumstances. This subsection delves into the qualities of leaders who excel at adaptive decision-making, providing practical strategies for embracing agility and resilience. By adopting an adaptive mindset, leaders position themselves to navigate the ever-evolving landscape of strategic ascendance.

7.3 The Inspirational Catalyst

Leaders who serve as inspirational catalysts ignite passion and commitment among their teams, creating a ripple effect that propels strategic endeavors forward. This section explores leadership styles that inspire and motivate, driving individuals and organizations to reach new heights.

Subsection 7.3.1: The Empowering Coach

Empowering coaches uplift and develop their teams, fostering a culture of continuous improvement. This subsection explores the principles of coaching leadership, providing insights into how leaders can empower others through mentorship, guidance, and skill development. Through practical exercises, readers gain tools to embody the empowering coach style in their strategic leadership approach.

Servant leadership centers on the idea of serving others as the primary focus of leadership. This subsection delves into the qualities of servant leaders, individuals who prioritize the well-being and growth of their teams. By embracing the principles of servant leadership, individuals cultivate a leadership style that contributes to the collective success of the organization.

7.4 The Collaborative Orchestrator

Collaborative orchestrators bring individuals together, harmonizing diverse talents and perspectives to achieve strategic goals. This section explores leadership styles that excel in collaboration, showcasing how leaders can foster a culture of teamwork and collective achievement.

Inclusive leaders champion diversity and create an environment where everyone feels valued and heard. This subsection explores the qualities of inclusive leaders and provides practical strategies for fostering inclusivity within teams and organizations. By embracing inclusive leadership, individuals contribute to a collaborative culture that enhances strategic ascendance.

Team builders excel at assembling and leading high-performing teams. This subsection delves into the strategies employed by effective team builders, offering insights into team dynamics, talent development, and creating a cohesive working environment. Through case studies and reflective exercises, readers gain tools to enhance their team-building skills for strategic success.

As we explore the panorama of leadership styles for strategic ascendance, we invite you to consider the nuanced art of leadership, recognizing that the most effective leaders are those who can adapt their styles to the demands of the strategic landscape. In the orchestration of success, leadership becomes the guiding melody that resonates with vision, adaptability, inspiration, and collaboration.

Section 2: Inspiring and Leading Teams to Success

In the alchemy of leadership, the ability to inspire and lead teams emerges as a transformative force, turning aspirations into collective achievements. This section explores the principles, strategies, and guiding principles for leaders seeking to inspire and lead teams to success on the journey of strategic ascendance.

7.5 The Essence of Team Leadership

Leading teams is an art that involves blending vision, collaboration, and motivation. In this section, we delve into the essence of team leadership, unraveling the qualities and strategies that distinguish leaders who inspire and guide teams toward success.

Subsection 7.5.1: Visionary Team Leadership

Visionary team leaders not only have a clear vision for the future but also instill that vision within their teams. This subsection explores the principles of visionary team leadership, emphasizing the importance of aligning team goals with the overarching strategic vision. Through case studies and practical insights, readers gain tools to inspire teams with a compelling vision that propels them toward strategic success.

Subsection 7.5.2: Creating a Culture of Collaboration

A culture of collaboration is the fertile soil in which team success takes root. This subsection delves into the strategies for creating and fostering a collaborative team culture. By emphasizing open communication, shared goals, and a sense of collective ownership, team leaders cultivate an environment where collaboration becomes a strategic advantage.

7.6 Strategies for Motivating and Engaging Teams

Motivation is the engine that drives teams toward their goals, and effective team leaders are adept at fueling this motivation. This section outlines actionable strategies for motivating and engaging teams in the pursuit of strategic success.

Subsection 7.6.1: Recognizing and Rewarding Contributions

Recognition and rewards are powerful motivators that fuel individual and team performance. This subsection explores the art of recognizing and rewarding contributions within teams, offering insights into how leaders can celebrate achievements, foster a positive team environment, and reinforce a culture of excellence.

Subsection 7.6.2: Tailoring Leadership to Individual and Team Needs

Effective team leadership involves understanding the unique needs and strengths of team members. This subsection provides strategies for tailoring leadership approaches to individual and team dynamics. By recognizing diverse strengths and preferences, team leaders can create a customized leadership approach that maximizes the potential of each team member.

7.7 Fostering Team Resilience and Adaptability

In the dynamic landscape of strategic endeavors, resilience and adaptability are essential qualities for teams. This section explores how team leaders can foster resilience and adaptability within their teams, ensuring they can navigate challenges and seize opportunities strategically.

Subsection 7.7.1: Building a Resilient Team Culture

Resilience is not just an individual quality; it can be woven into the fabric of team culture. This subsection delves into the strategies for building a resilient team culture, emphasizing the importance of embracing setbacks as learning opportunities, fostering a growth mindset, and cultivating a sense of collective resilience.

Subsection 7.7.2: Navigating Change with Team Agility

Adaptability is a strategic asset in the face of change. This subsection explores how team leaders can cultivate agility within their teams, ensuring they can navigate change with flexibility and strategic acumen.

By fostering a culture of continuous learning and adaptability, team leaders position their teams for success in dynamic environments.

As we explore the realm of inspiring and leading teams to success, we invite you to consider the profound impact of effective team leadership on the journey of strategic ascendance. In the symphony of leadership alchemy, team leaders become the conductors who orchestrate collective success, harmonizing the diverse talents and energies of individuals toward a shared vision of strategic triumph.

Chapter 8: The Ethical Tapestry

Section 1: The Ethical Dimension of Strategic Success

In the intricate tapestry of strategic ascendance, the ethical dimension weaves through every thread, shaping the character and enduring success of individuals and organizations. This section explores the pivotal role of ethics in the strategic landscape, offering insights, principles, and reflections on how ethical considerations contribute to a sustainable and principled journey to success.

8.1 The Moral Compass of Strategic Thinking

Ethics is the moral compass that guides strategic thinking, ensuring that success is not only achieved but sustained with integrity. In this section, we delve into the foundational principles of ethical decision-making and the profound impact it has on the strategic journey.

Subsection 8.1.1: Integrity as the Cornerstone of Strategic Success

Integrity is the cornerstone upon which strategic success is built. This subsection explores the strategic significance of integrity, emphasizing how individuals and organizations can cultivate a culture of honesty, transparency, and ethical conduct. Through case studies and reflective exercises, readers gain insights into the ways in which integrity becomes the bedrock of enduring success.

Subsection 8.1.2: Balancing Ambition with Ethical Considerations

Ambition is the driving force behind strategic endeavors, but its alignment with ethical considerations is paramount. This subsection delves into the delicate balance between ambition and ethics, providing strategies for individuals and organizations to pursue their goals with vigor while ensuring that ethical principles remain at the forefront. By navigating this balance, strategic thinkers cultivate a reputation for principled success.

8.2 Transparency and Accountability in Strategic Conduct

Transparency and accountability are not just virtues; they are strategic imperatives that foster trust and resilience. This section explores the role of transparency and accountability in the ethical dimension of strategic conduct, offering insights into their transformative impact on individual and organizational success.

Subsection 8.2.1: The Strategic Power of Transparent Communication

Transparent communication is the bedrock of trust in strategic relationships. This subsection explores the strategic power of transparent communication, emphasizing the role it plays in building and maintaining trust with stakeholders. By adopting a commitment to open and honest communication, individuals and organizations fortify the ethical fabric of their strategic endeavors.

Subsection 8.2.2: Embracing Accountability for Ethical Decision-Making

Accountability is the crucible in which ethical decisions are tested and affirmed. This subsection delves into the principles of accountability for ethical decision-making, providing strategies for individuals and organizations to hold themselves responsible for the consequences of their actions. By embracing accountability, strategic thinkers ensure that ethical considerations are not merely theoretical but integral to the execution of their strategies.

8.3 The Social Responsibility of Strategic Success

Strategic success extends beyond individual or organizational boundaries; it carries a social responsibility. This section explores the ethical considerations related to social responsibility in strategic conduct, highlighting the transformative impact of strategic endeavors on communities and society at large.

Subsection 8.3.1: Contributing to Sustainable and Responsible Practices

Sustainability and responsible practices are ethical imperatives in the strategic landscape. This subsection explores how individuals and organizations can contribute to sustainable development and responsible business practices. By aligning strategic goals with a commitment to environmental, social, and governance (ESG) principles, strategic thinkers become architects of positive change.

Subsection 8.3.2: Nurturing Ethical Leadership in Organizational Culture

Ethical leadership is not just a personal attribute; it is a cultural cornerstone. This subsection delves into the strategies for nurturing ethical leadership within organizational culture, emphasizing the role of leaders in setting the tone for ethical conduct. By fostering a culture that values ethical decision-making, organizations contribute to a broader societal framework of responsible and principled success.

As we explore the ethical dimension of strategic success, we invite you to view ethics not as a constraint but as a catalyst for enduring triumph. In the ethical tapestry of strategic ascendance, individuals and organizations become stewards of a legacy that transcends mere accomplishments, resonating with principles and values that stand the test of time.

Section 2: Achieving Ambitious Goals with Integrity

In the pursuit of strategic ascendance, the alignment of ambitious goals with unwavering integrity forms the crucible in which enduring success is forged. This section explores the principles, strategies, and transformative potential of achieving ambitious goals with a steadfast commitment to ethical conduct.

8.4 The Harmony of Ambition and Integrity

Ambition is the heartbeat of strategic endeavors, propelling individuals and organizations toward ambitious goals. In this section, we delve into the delicate yet potent harmony of ambition and integrity, showcasing how these two elements can coalesce to create a symphony of success.

Subsection 8.4.1: Defining Ambitious Goals with Strategic Clarity

Ambitious goals, when defined with strategic clarity, become beacons that guide the journey to success. This subsection explores the principles of setting ambitious yet ethically sound goals, emphasizing the importance of aligning goals with a clear strategic vision. Through case studies and practical insights, readers gain tools to articulate goals that inspire progress while maintaining a commitment to ethical conduct.

Subsection 8.4.2: The Ethical Framework for Goal Pursuit

The pursuit of ambitious goals requires a robust ethical framework that serves as a compass in the face of challenges. This subsection delves into the elements of an ethical framework for goal pursuit, providing strategies for individuals and organizations to integrate ethical considerations into every stage of their strategic journey. By adopting a principled approach, strategic thinkers fortify the foundation upon which ambitious goals are achieved with integrity.

8.5 Strategies for Ethical Goal Execution

Executing ambitious goals ethically involves more than intention; it requires strategic approaches that prioritize integrity at every step. This section outlines actionable strategies for individuals and organizations committed to achieving ambitious goals with unwavering ethical conduct.

Subsection 8.5.1: Transparent Stakeholder Engagement

Stakeholders are integral partners in the pursuit of ambitious goals. This subsection explores the strategic importance of transparent stakeholder engagement, emphasizing the role of open communication, collaboration, and shared understanding. By fostering a transparent dialogue with stakeholders, individuals and organizations cultivate an environment of trust that sustains ethical goal execution.

Subsection 8.5.2: Ethical Decision-Making in Dynamic Environments

The landscape of goal execution is dynamic, presenting unforeseen challenges that demand ethical decision-making. This subsection delves into the strategies for making ethical decisions in dynamic environments, providing insights into adaptability, resilience, and maintaining ethical principles in the face of changing circumstances. By embedding ethical decision-making into the fabric of goal execution, strategic thinkers navigate challenges with integrity.

8.6 Navigating Challenges with Ethical Resilience

Ambitious goals are often accompanied by challenges, and ethical resilience is the strategic shield that ensures unwavering commitment to integrity. This section explores the principles and strategies for navigating challenges with ethical resilience, showcasing how individuals and organizations can transform setbacks into opportunities for ethical growth.

Subsection 8.6.1: Learning from Ethical Setbacks*

Ethical setbacks are not defeats; they are lessons in resilience and growth. This subsection delves into the transformative potential of learning from ethical setbacks, providing insights into how individuals and organizations can extract valuable lessons from challenges. By adopting a mindset of continuous improvement, strategic thinkers turn setbacks into strategic opportunities for ethical refinement.

*Subsection 8.6.2: Integrating Ethical Reflection into Goal Evaluation**

Goal evaluation is incomplete without ethical reflection. This subsection explores the strategic importance of integrating ethical reflection into the evaluation of ambitious goals, emphasizing the role of introspection, feedback, and continuous ethical improvement. By incorporating ethical reflection into the strategic process, individuals and organizations ensure that their achievements are not only ambitious but enduring.

As we explore the tapestry of achieving ambitious goals with integrity, we invite you to consider that the true measure of success is not merely the attainment of goals but the manner in which those goals are achieved. In the symphony of strategic ascendance, the pursuit of ambitious goals with unwavering integrity becomes a harmonious melody that resonates with lasting impact and principled triumph.

Chapter 9: The Ascendant Horizon

Section 1: Long-Term Strategies for Continuous Ascendance

As the journey of strategic ascendance unfolds, the horizon extends beyond immediate triumphs to embrace the enduring pursuit of success. This section explores the principles, methodologies, and visionary strategies for individuals and organizations committed to continuous ascendance over the long term.

9.1 The Visionary Canvas of Long-Term Thinking

Long-term strategies are not mere plans; they are visionary canvases that paint the trajectory of sustained success. In this section, we delve into the principles and transformative power of long-term thinking, showcasing how individuals and organizations can sculpt their future with strategic foresight.

Subsection 9.1.1: Articulating a Compelling Long-Term Vision

A compelling long-term vision is the lodestar that guides strategic decisions and actions. This subsection explores the art of articulating a vision that extends beyond immediate goals, encapsulating a future that aligns with overarching values and aspirations. Through case studies and practical insights, readers gain tools to craft a visionary narrative that inspires continuous ascendance.

Subsection 9.1.2: Strategic Foresight as a Compass for Decision-Making

Strategic foresight is the compass that navigates the journey of continuous ascendance. This subsection delves into the principles of strategic foresight, providing strategies for individuals and organizations to anticipate trends, identify opportunities, and make informed decisions that contribute to long-term success. By cultivating a proactive stance toward the future, strategic thinkers position themselves to navigate the evolving landscape with agility.

9.2 Adaptive Excellence in Long-Term Strategies

Long-term success requires not just strategic planning but adaptive excellence that responds to dynamic environments. This section explores the principles and strategies for cultivating adaptive excellence in long-term strategies, showcasing how individuals and organizations can thrive in the face of change.

Subsection 9.2.1: The Iterative Approach to Strategy Refinement

Long-term strategies benefit from an iterative approach that allows for continuous refinement. This subsection explores the principles of iterative strategy refinement, providing insights into how individuals and organizations can embrace a dynamic process of learning, adjusting, and improving their strategies over time. By adopting an iterative mindset, strategic thinkers transform challenges into opportunities for strategic growth.

Subsection 9.2.2: Nurturing a Culture of Continuous Learning

Continuous learning is the lifeblood of adaptive excellence. This subsection delves into the strategies for nurturing a culture of continuous learning within organizations, emphasizing the role of curiosity, experimentation, and knowledge-sharing. By fostering an environment that values ongoing learning, strategic thinkers cultivate adaptability that becomes a cornerstone of long-term success.

9.3 Building Resilience into the Fabric of Long-Term Strategies

Resilience is not just a response to challenges; it is a strategic asset that fortifies long-term success. This section explores the principles and strategies for building resilience into the fabric of long-term strategies, showcasing how individuals and organizations can navigate uncertainties with strategic strength.

Subsection 9.3.1: Anticipating and Mitigating Risks Strategically

Strategic risk management is integral to building resilience. This subsection explores the principles of anticipating and mitigating risks strategically, providing insights into how individuals and organizations can identify potential challenges and proactively develop strategies for resilience. By integrating risk management into the strategic process, strategic thinkers position themselves to navigate disruptions with strategic strength.

Subsection 9.3.2: Cultivating Organizational Agility for Strategic Resilience

Organizational agility is the strategic shield against uncertainties. This subsection delves into the strategies for cultivating organizational agility, emphasizing the importance of flexibility, adaptability, and proactive decision-making. By embedding agility into the organizational culture, strategic thinkers ensure that their long-term strategies are not just robust but resilient in the face of evolving challenges.

As we explore the realm of long-term strategies for continuous ascendance, we invite you to consider that enduring success is not a destination but a dynamic journey. In the grand tapestry of strategic ascendance, individuals and organizations become architects of their future, shaping a narrative of continuous growth, adaptation, and triumph.

Section 2: Managing Success and Avoiding Complacency

As success unfolds on the ascendant horizon, the challenge becomes not just achieving triumphs but navigating the complexities of sustained success. This section explores the principles, strategies, and proactive measures for effectively managing success and avoiding the pitfalls of complacency in the continuous journey of ascendance.

9.4 The Dynamics of Managing Success

Managing success is an art that requires strategic finesse, adaptability, and a keen awareness of the evolving landscape. In this section, we delve into the dynamics of managing success, showcasing how individuals and organizations can navigate the nuances of triumph to ensure continuous growth.

Subsection 9.4.1: Strategic Reflection on Achievements*

Strategic reflection is the cornerstone of managing success effectively. This subsection explores the principles of strategic reflection, providing insights into how individuals and organizations can assess their achievements, identify key learnings, and refine their strategies for continuous improvement. By fostering a culture of introspection, strategic thinkers elevate success management to a dynamic and iterative process.

Subsection 9.4.2: Aligning Success with Evolving Goals*

As goals evolve, success management requires a dynamic alignment with these shifting objectives. This subsection delves into the strategies for aligning success with evolving goals, emphasizing the importance of reassessing priorities, adjusting benchmarks, and ensuring that success remains congruent with the broader strategic vision. By proactively adapting to changing goals, individuals and organizations position themselves for sustained ascendance.

9.5 The Pitfalls of Complacency in Success

Complacency lurks as a silent threat in the wake of success, and recognizing its pitfalls is crucial for maintaining strategic momentum. This section explores the nuances of complacency, offering insights, warnings, and strategies to preemptively address this potential impediment to continuous ascendance.

*Subsection 9.5.1: Identifying Indicators of Complacency**

Complacency often disguises itself in subtle indicators that require astute observation. This subsection explores the signs and indicators of complacency, providing individuals and organizations with the tools to recognize when success might be veering toward stagnation. By staying vigilant to these indicators, strategic thinkers can intervene proactively to maintain a trajectory of ascendance.

*Subsection 9.5.2: Strategies for Complacency Prevention**

Preventing complacency involves strategic interventions that disrupt the status quo. This subsection delves into the strategies for preventing complacency, offering insights into how individuals and organizations can infuse innovation, continuous learning, and a culture of challenge into their success management approaches. By implementing proactive measures, strategic thinkers inoculate themselves against the seductive allure of complacency.

9.6 Fostering a Culture of Continuous Improvement

In the landscape of continuous ascendance, success is not a destination but a waypoint in an ongoing journey of improvement. This section explores the principles and strategies for fostering a culture of continuous improvement, ensuring that success becomes a springboard for even greater achievements.

Subsection 9.6.1: Integrating Feedback Loops for Strategic Growth*

Feedback is the currency of continuous improvement. This subsection explores the integration of feedback loops into success management, emphasizing the strategic importance of soliciting, analyzing, and acting upon feedback from stakeholders. By cultivating an environment that values feedback, strategic thinkers propel themselves toward perpetual growth.

Subsection 9.6.2: Instilling a Growth Mindset in Success Management*

A growth mindset is the catalyst for sustained ascendance. This subsection delves into the strategies for instilling a growth mindset within success management, providing insights into how individuals and organizations can embrace challenges, view setbacks as opportunities for learning, and cultivate a resilient attitude toward continuous improvement. By fostering a growth mindset, strategic thinkers lay the groundwork for perpetual success in the dynamic landscape of ascendance.

As we explore the intricacies of managing success and avoiding complacency, we invite you to view success not as a static achievement but as a dynamic force that requires strategic stewardship. In the symphony of ascendant horizons, success management becomes the art of orchestrating continuous growth, adaptability, and triumph.

Conclusion: A Call to Action

As we reach the culmination of this exploration into the art and science of strategic ascendance, the tapestry of insights and strategies unveiled throughout these pages converges into a compelling call to action. Crafting your unique path to strategic ascendance is not a passive endeavor; it is a dynamic journey that requires intention, adaptability, and a resolute commitment to continuous growth.

Embrace Strategic Mindfulness:

Strategic ascendance begins with a heightened awareness of your surroundings, goals, and the ever-shifting landscape of opportunities and challenges. Embrace strategic mindfulness as a daily practice, honing your ability to observe, analyze, and discern the nuances that shape your strategic journey.

Define Your Vision and Values:

Crafting your unique path requires a clear vision that transcends immediate objectives—a vision that resonates with your values and aspirations. Define your vision with precision, anchoring it in the principles and values that serve as guiding stars on your journey to ascendance.

Cultivate Adaptive Excellence:

In the dynamic terrain of strategic endeavors, adaptability is not just a virtue; it is a strategic imperative. Cultivate adaptive excellence by embracing change, learning from setbacks, and approaching challenges with resilience. Adaptability is the secret sauce that transforms obstacles into stepping stones toward ascendance.

Build Strategic Networks:

Your journey is not solitary; it is woven into the fabric of connections and collaborations. Build strategic networks intentionally, recognizing the transformative power of relationships. Networks are not just resources; they are strategic allies that amplify your capacity for innovation, learning, and collective success.

Navigate Challenges with Foresight:

Challenges are not roadblocks but opportunities for strategic refinement. Navigate challenges with foresight, leveraging strategic thinking to anticipate, mitigate, and transform obstacles into strategic advantages. Foresight is the compass that guides you through the complexities of the ascendant journey.

Sustain Ethical Principles:

Integrity is the compass that ensures your ascent is not only high but principled. Sustain ethical principles as the bedrock of your strategic endeavors. Align your goals with ethical considerations, communicate transparently, and embrace social responsibility. Ethical conduct is not just a choice; it is the essence of enduring success.

Inspire and Lead with Purpose:

In the orchestration of ascendance, leadership becomes the guiding melody. Inspire and lead with purpose, recognizing that true leadership extends beyond individual accomplishments to empower and uplift others. Cultivate leadership styles that align with your vision, creating a harmonious symphony of collaboration and inspiration.

Commit to Continuous Improvement:

Success is not a static achievement; it is a dynamic journey of continuous improvement. Commit to perpetual growth by embracing feedback, instilling a growth mindset, and fostering a culture of continuous improvement. The pursuit of excellence is not a destination; it is an ongoing commitment to surpassing your best self.

Avoid the Sirens of Complacency:

As you ascend, beware of the seductive whispers of complacency. Actively manage success by staying vigilant to its subtle pitfalls. Identify indicators of complacency, implement strategies for prevention, and foster a culture of challenge and innovation. Complacency is the silent adversary of ascendance; resilience and adaptability are its antidotes.

Craft Your Unique Narrative:

Finally, craft your unique narrative of strategic ascendance. Your journey is not a replication of others; it is an original composition that unfolds with every strategic decision, every adaptation, and every triumph. Embrace the uniqueness of your path, and let it resonate with purpose, authenticity, and enduring success.

The call to action is now yours. The canvas is blank, waiting for the strokes of intention, the hues of adaptability, and the brilliance of strategic acumen. As you embark on your unique path to strategic ascendance, may each step be guided by the wisdom gained from these pages, and may your journey be a symphony of strategic triumphs that resonate across the landscapes of success.

Appendix: Additional Resources and Tools

As you embark on your journey of strategic ascendance, consider this collection of resources and tools as companions to enhance your understanding, refine your strategies, and amplify your capabilities. This curated list includes books, frameworks, and platforms that delve deeper into various aspects of strategic thinking, leadership, and continuous improvement.

Books on Strategic Thinking and Leadership:

1. *Good Strategy Bad Strategy: The Difference and Why It Matters* by Richard Rumelt
2. *The Lean Startup: How Today's Entrepreneurs Use Continuous Innovation to Create Radically Successful Businesses* by Eric Ries
3. *Drive: The Surprising Truth About What Motivates Us* by Daniel H. Pink
4. *Thinking, Fast and Slow* by Daniel Kahneman
5. *Leaders Eat Last: Why Some Teams Pull Together and Others Don't* by Simon Sinek
6. *The Innovator's Dilemma: When New Technologies Cause Great Firms to Fail* by Clayton M. Christensen
7. *Mindset: The New Psychology of Success* by Carol S. Dweck
8. *Blue Ocean Strategy: How to Create Uncontested Market Space and Make Competition Irrelevant* by W. Chan Kim and Renée Mauborgne

Strategic Frameworks and Models:

1. **SWOT Analysis:**
   - A classic framework for identifying Strengths, Weaknesses, Opportunities, and Threats.
2. **PESTLE Analysis:**
   - A comprehensive tool for understanding the external macro-environmental factors that can impact your organization.

3. **Balanced Scorecard:**
   - A strategic performance management tool that aligns business activities to the organization's vision and strategy.
4. **Ansoff Matrix:**
   - A matrix that helps organizations identify growth strategies by exploring product and market combinations.
5. **Business Model Canvas:**
   - A visual framework for developing, describing, and pivoting business models.

Online Platforms and Communities:

1. **Harvard Business Review (HBR):**
   - An authoritative source for business insights, research, and thought leadership.
2. **Strategy+Business:**
   - A publication providing strategic insights, ideas, and practical advice for business leaders.
3. **LinkedIn Learning:**
   - Offers courses on various business and leadership topics, including strategic thinking and management.
4. **MindTools:**
   - A platform providing practical resources to help individuals excel in their careers, including tools for strategic planning.
5. **Strategic Management Society:**
   - An international society that brings together academics, business practitioners, and consultants to advance the field of strategic management.

These resources and tools are not exhaustive but serve as a starting point for further exploration and development. Remember, the journey of strategic ascendance is a continuous learning process, and these materials can be valuable companions on your path to success.

Case Studies in Strategic Ascendance

Real-world examples provide invaluable insights into the complexities and triumphs of strategic ascendance. The following case studies illuminate diverse paths taken by individuals and organizations, showcasing the principles, challenges, and strategic acumen that contribute to their ascent.

1. Apple Inc.: The Innovation Trailblazer

Overview: Apple Inc. stands as an iconic example of strategic ascendance through relentless innovation. From the introduction of the Macintosh in the 1980s to the revolutionary iPhone and beyond, Apple has consistently disrupted industries, redefined user experiences, and maintained a remarkable brand allure.

Key Takeaways:

- Innovation as a Core Value: Apple's commitment to innovation is embedded in its organizational DNA. The company continually pushes boundaries, introducing products that redefine markets.
- Ecosystem Synergy: Apple's ecosystem, comprising hardware, software, and services, creates a seamless user experience. The synergy between products strengthens customer loyalty and drives sustained success.

2. Netflix: Streaming into the Future

Overview: Netflix transformed the entertainment industry by evolving from a DVD rental-by-mail service to a global streaming powerhouse. The company's strategic ascendance is characterized by a bold shift in business model, investment in original content, and a focus on data-driven personalization.

Key Takeaways:

- Adaptability to Technological Shifts: Netflix recognized the shift from physical to digital consumption early on and strategically positioned itself at the forefront of the streaming revolution.

- Data-Driven Decision-Making: The use of data analytics to understand viewer preferences has been instrumental in shaping content creation, personalized recommendations, and strategic decision-making.

3. Toyota: Driving Efficiency and Quality

Overview: Toyota's ascent to become a global automotive giant is rooted in the principles of lean manufacturing and continuous improvement. The Toyota Production System (TPS) is a benchmark for operational excellence, emphasizing efficiency, quality, and waste reduction.

Key Takeaways:

- Kaizen Philosophy: Toyota's commitment to Kaizen, or continuous improvement, permeates its organizational culture. Every employee is encouraged to contribute ideas for incremental improvements.
- Supply Chain Resilience: Toyota's strategic ascendance is linked to its robust supply chain management. The company prioritizes long-term relationships with suppliers, fostering a network of partners committed to shared success.

4. Alibaba Group: Navigating E-Commerce Seas

Overview: Alibaba Group, founded by Jack Ma, is a Chinese multinational conglomerate that has become a global e-commerce giant. The company's strategic ascendance is marked by innovation in online marketplaces, digital finance, cloud computing, and more.

Key Takeaways:

- Ecosystem Diversification: Alibaba's success is not limited to e-commerce; the company has strategically diversified into various sectors, creating an interconnected ecosystem of businesses.
- Global Expansion with Local Sensibility: Alibaba's global expansion has been characterized by an understanding of local markets and a commitment to tailoring services to meet diverse cultural and business needs.

These case studies offer a glimpse into the multifaceted nature of strategic ascendance. They underscore the importance of adaptability, innovation, continuous improvement, and a visionary approach to navigating the complexities of today's dynamic business landscape.

www.ingramcontent.com/pod-product-compliance
Lightning Source LLC
Chambersburg PA
CBHW031329250726
48656CB00005B/2039